After the Splendid Display

Wesleyan New Poets

After the Splendid Display

Don Bogen

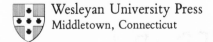 Wesleyan University Press
Middletown, Connecticut

For Cathryn

Copyright © 1986 by Don Bogen

Some of the poems in this book appeared previously: "After the Splendid Display," "Pasadena," "Peddler," *The American Poetry Review;* "Leaving California," *Clifton;* "Bay Window in a Rented House," *Correspondances;* "Policies," *Indiana Review;* "The Last Installment," "Net," *The Kenyon Review;* "Pioneer Square," *The Nation;* "Glass Music," "The House Destroyed by Fire," *The New Republic;* "Family Album," *The North American Review;* "Crawling Home," "Learning to Clam," "A Postcard from St. Petersburg," *The Paris Review;* "A Scholar Gazing at a Flight of Birds," "Swan Song," *Ploughshares;* "Reggae Music," *Sidewinder;* "The All-Night Rumba," *Southern Poetry Review;* "A Priest of Aphrodisias," "Winter House," *Stand;* "At the Concert," "Klumb's Rise," *The Threepenny Review.*

The epigraph to "Reggae Music" is from a radio interview with Bob Marley.

All inquiries and permission requests should be addressed to the Publisher, Wesleyan University Press, 110 Mt. Vernon Street, Middletown, Connecticut 06457.

Distributed by Harper & Row Publishers, Keystone Industrial Park, Scranton, Pennsylvania 18512.

LIBRARY OF CONGRESS CATALOGING IN PUBLICATION DATA
Bogen, Don.
  After the splendid display.
  (Wesleyan new poets)
  I. Title. II. Series.
PS3552.04337A69 1986   811'.54   85-8826
ISBN 0-8195-2127-2 (alk. paper)
ISBN 0-8195-1128-5 (pbk. : alk. paper)

Manufactured in the United States of America

First Edition

WESLEYAN NEW POETS

Contents

I

Crawling Home

At the end of the nineteenth century
things got wiggly.
You tried to make photographs and the camera wiggled.
The dancers looked fuzzy, half-haloed.
You noticed the cast-iron railing
you were leaning on wiggled too.
Strands of smoke from your Gauloises
writhed up and twined in the air.
When you went outside to paint what you saw,
what you saw was wiggly light.

And people in wiggly light,
chatting, strolling, rowing in a shimmering park.
Taffeta ruffles, hat ribbons, velvet bow ties
wiggled at you in a breeze that was always there.
Black caterpillars squirmed under noses.
Spit curls wormed down from hairlines.
Half-naked Isadora Duncan
did her snake dance,
while the graying heir apparent to the Austro-Hungarian Empire
made his most gracious bow.

A bullet sliced clean through the delicate
ripples of skin round his throat.
He twitched, died, went stiff as a brick,
and got buried in an eight-foot velvet box.
Meanwhile frock-coated diplomats chopped
the still air. Fresh troughs terraced
hillsides, cutting the plains into squares.
Crosses were already jutting up behind the fronts
when you began to crawl from trench to trench
slowly, in a straight line.

A Corner

The planted sycamores are budding again
in the park laid out in front of the Milner Hotel.
Their new shoots, as light almost as tarnished bronze,
reflect on the smoked glass of the Milner Restaurant
like rags of cloud across a mud-swollen stream.
The days when a man might reach toward the purchase of a whole block
are gone. A rich name splayed across brick
chips. Behind the gilt-lettered windows of the Milner Bar & Grill
the worn-out employees of the man's grandchildren
stare at the trees or the dull heroic statue of Garfield.
Since he was a shorter man, the artist cast him one and a half times
human size. His right fist clutches a roll of green
documents in a sculptured motif reminiscent of
the sheaf of arrows snared in the eagle's claw.
The empty hand gestures to the trees, the mouth caught open
in a flower of oratory. He stands for the little man,
the gold standard, full disclosure, and all the glories
of an expanding century. There is a molded swell
beneath the wide-lapelled frock coat buttoned high
on the breast and, peeking out, a prim bronze vest.

Glass Music

*Herr von Mesmer, at whose house we lunched on
Monday, played to us on Miss Davies' harmonica
or glass instrument, and played very well. It cost
him about 50 ducats and it is very beautifully
made. He is the only person in Vienna who has
learnt it and he possesses a much finer instrument
than Miss Davies does. Wolfgang too has played
upon it. How I should like to have one!*
—LEOPOLD MOZART, 1773

Imagine Mozart: his porcelain cheeks
gone paler still, those orbs of eye glazed, one lip
trembling like the score in his palm. He aches
with beauty, but the music will not stop
till it holds him as a god could, with one look,
then lets him drop. He yearns to offer up
a sweet piece of his own for what he heard
played on an instrument he couldn't afford.

Tender-eyed Anton Mesmer easily tires
of fame. To lull some people into a doze—
what science is in that, what skill? He wonders,
touching the rich instrument, what he does
to earn all this: the jeweled pendants, white chairs
light as if carved in heaven, the gleaming rows
of keys—like so many gifts. With a sigh
he picks one final toccata to play.

And Mozart? Mesmerized. Ghost-tones ring the room
as if it were a goblet, while his host thinks
of work, how it's all a kind of play—some
diddle pendulums, some scribble notes. Lank
as a trinket, the guest is dangling from
his dream: this music of the spheres. When it sinks
at Mesmer's touch to its deep, closing phrase,
Mozart can only thank him with his eyes.

Imagine the chain of gifts: Mozart's sweet art,
Mesmer's gaze, his instrument—the best
in all Vienna—its tones that seem to start
in heaven or nowhere . . . and behind this list
the fat inventor: Ben Franklin, in a shirt
soured with sweat, linking chain drives to shafts.
He pulls a crank, listens as glass music sifts
from air, this man who doesn't believe in gifts.

A Scholar Gazing at a Flight of Birds

Calm, cross-legged on his narrow ledge
of fifteenth-century Chinese bureaucracy,
a scholar gazing at a flight of birds

observes what he already knows. That those wings
are quick as brush strokes is self-evident.
Or that the mist is swelling just like water

dropped on rice paper. There is a moon, of course,
fat and pale as an old poet's belly, which will rise,
shine on a pool and be toasted with rice wine.

Everything the scholar sees is arranged.
The scholar Wang Yun painted it that way.
He set the man on his outlandish cliff,

dribbled in fog, stuck the scrub pines out
perpendicular to the standard fist of rock,
dabbled on a spray of teahouse lights,

and waited for the wash of air to dry.
The last strokes, reaching out to that squiggle of birds,
were easy, older than the trees themselves.

His hand leapt centuries. His mind wandered.
I suppose he may have been thinking of the time
he sat half-drunk on a ledge in Szechuan

not at all like this one, or old friends
the empire supported and scattered, or promotion.
Blotting the clouds, he didn't need to care

which path of emulation the new piece took.
Sublime masters nodded behind the right moves
like portly household gods. A day's work done,

he may have gone off in the moonlight, leaving the cliff,
scholar, and birds fading into calligraphy
across the left-hand corner of the sky.

Pasadena

Screech of a cockatoo in early smog—
more a haze really, bundled at the knees
of the mountains like a driving blanket.
Ice plant and dusty ivy. Vague succulents
ruminating in pots. A purple curtain
steeped all day in sun. In 1910
the grounds are as broad as the century
and half as wild.
                        Hot springs and séances.
From the descending incline railroad car
the house grows as the groves begin to shrink—
cottage, mission, castle, then cottage again
when the driver unlatches the gate. Old air
cool in the shut rooms. The small parade of help.
Exotics flourish in a walled garden,
obscure palms and rumors:
                        The sacked footman
stroking her pale thighs in the carriage house
had his moment of joy. Her man-sized pet
gorilla got loose and romped among the bungalows
a scandalous week. His trim cage at the zoo
grows a jungle of Egyptiana on its front.
The gardener turns Japanese. Once a week
he makes his quick snip.
                        Elusive, half-retired,
the mountains are drifting off under a soiled cloud.
Stucco numbs the estate. Each new plot
has a lemon tree, a tiled garage, and a three-
bedroom hacienda with a bird feeder.
In moments of uproarious flickered light
a young man, staid and manic, is racing down
the boulevard ahead of a herd of steers.

A Postcard from St. Petersburg

The best footman's good
at sweeping up your broken glass,
has a tear for every occasion, knows
the weather and has committed
several hundred incomprehensible proverbs
to memory.
    The best cook's
gruff, beats you out of the kitchen
with a wooden spoon, got
fat from sipping at the gravy and plans
to stay that way.
    The best
groom's mute, with eyes like mournful
chestnuts.
    The best butler
mumbles in his pantry, is large enough
to frighten off your unwanted guests, sips
vodka at New Year's and blinks
when your niece Vasilisa waltzes out the night
with the young officer
      who will whisk
her off, doffing his hat to the serfs
as the troika flies to the old driver's
whip and they slide away into a future as safe
as snow.

Winter House

When the fire won't start, we turn the furnace up.
The logs, all charred bark blanketing pure hearts
of winter, sprawl in the cast-iron grate—
they might as well be chunks of dirt. And the door
might as well be sand, for all the good
it does. Night wind breaks in, cool as a thief
hacksawing through at the crack.

                                 It makes me think
of North Dakota. Now I'm beginning to feel
why your grandfather left. That one-room sod
house like a cellar without a house
on top, a white lump on a whiter plain,
the east wall lean-to where the summer kitchen
kept filling up with snow.

                           Where could he go
but California? There he closed his life
growing apricots across a straw-colored hill,
more than he could eat or chose to sell.
I never tasted them, but now I bet
just one tart half-ball on my tongue would do:
a mouth full of sun.

                          Or maybe full
of earth. I know he bragged about the time
his father conned a neighbor out of an ox,
to beat a life from the dirt. And yet you say
he'd rail against *those rascals* everywhere.
I'll never figure him out. I know the scenes—
cold plain and orchard—

                         still the core resists,
tough as a seed. But it's getting warmer now,
I can hear our furnace grunting on over the noise
of your work in the kitchen. The hot breeze
rises from the cellar through the arms
of pipe and warms us in our different rooms.
We'll let the logs dry for another fire.

The Last Installment

Remember our lamp, its frowzy Victorian hat
of a shade? Nights in that drafty stained-glass parlor
I'd read aloud in the fringed glow while you sewed.
We might have been someone's great-grandparents, or characters

in those fat books. Imagine our ancestors caught in them through
the long dark sea of the nineteenth century,
coming back month after month like letters home
from the Empire's most distant outpost. The day

is bright. Master is sitting chatting in the sitting room
and has called for early tea. I fancy the daughter
of the vicar has caught his quick eye. Outside, the broad heath
glowers as always. I spied someone poaching over there,

your lordship, grouse hunting he were, out beneath
last night's full moon. Good work, Barker, do keep
us alerted. In the shop at the curve of High Street
they are ringing a small bell for me. I want it to stop,

I don't want to bring in the great bolt of silk that
is taller than I shall ever be. Let the dance fail,
the heroine weep in last year's gown. Let the ship
sink, all its letters lost at sea, at the crazy wheel

the cabin boy at last. And our ancestors stumbling up
from steerage, blinking, in the cold salt light
of a dim empire of words, gathered by the crossing-sweep
for the factory girl so lovely and illiterate.

II

After the Splendid Display

What sport shall we devise here in this garden
To drive away the heavy thought of care?

After the splendid display at the rajah's parade grounds —
the horse marines so dashing, the band and guard, those delightful
decorated elephants — we strolled out under parasols to the yard,
each on an officer's arm, to attend the match. White
tables, boys bringing pitchers of quinine water — the heat,
you understand — sliced limes and gin for the gentlemen. The countess
wore that diamond brooch I must admit I envied.
In the interval one of the players approached me. I thought
it odd to see such a handsome young lieutenant in white
Indian cotton. He will meet Papa. Oh, my dearest friend,
I can scarcely explain to myself the secret flights of my
heart since our arrival, its springs and turns, — it is a very tennis-ball.

*   *   *

Tennis anyone? Todd always had been something
of a fool. Not one of us. That ridiculous Bentley,
his diamond tiepin, that "class of ought nine" camaraderie
just would not do. On the courts, of course, he sported
the finest whites, and the ducks he put on after his lengthy showers
fairly dazzled. But he couldn't hit the ball. And he didn't
hit it off well with the ladies either, always getting left behind
in clubs where the gin tasted like sen-sen and the band was flat.
Ted, now Ted was a regular guy, really white. We'd start
with a couple of quick ones over at Ted's place. There was old Ted,
half-mincing, blind, swinging a bottle of fizz
by the neck. Tennis anyone? Oh, could he kid, and he
could make the girls squeal. He knew all the best uptown clubs
and once cadged a reefer from the drummer at the Lenox Hotel.

*   *   *

The women are playing for cigarettes on TV.
We have the best seats, with a three-foot eye
sharper than the lineman's, our eight-packs,
Cheez-its, and instant replay. In the back
the spectators are melting as we watch—
they envy us, I bet, more with each stretch
and uncomfortable wriggle, each blow
of blind sun off the racket handles. Now
one of the cameras picks up the server:
the sweet blonde underdog. It is the serve
she has to make. Cut to shot of worried
young face. A slow pan up the legs, the gemmed
garter of sweat on each tanned thigh, then rise
with the ball and body rising into its poise
and that perfect swing that lets everyone see
she's come a long way baby.

*   *   *

Vanderbilt University, 1978.
Davis Cup: United States vs.
South Africa

The winners are always the ones
with the best strokes. It
is obvious in the pool
or in bed or on the trimmed
lawns and lined clay
of a place like Nashville.
But consider other strokes:
the gem cutter splitting
money from a stone, the
camera's caress, the way
a deft hand gripping
the blade can write a name

in flesh, a stroke of
luck, stroke of the winner coming
down on the white ball, stroke
of the whip, and pick stroke,
the black hand plucking
diamonds from the mine.

Net

When they step out from apartments facing the park
a little awning goes a ways with them.
Carpet massages their soles. A uniform
stands ready to call them a cab. When they start
their slow stroll down the street, up float some
friendly windows showing off the art
of hand-painted porcelain, clothes — a shirt
with a name sewn on, some silk — a dressed ham.
In the delight of day they take their ease,
and the world shimmers around them like a net
of light. All things are linked: those mounted police,
that man with balloons tied on his wrist, the pet
Weimaraner they love. Lank, beautiful,
he drifts ahead on his strap like a gray sail.

Folk Tale

So the folk they wander in the mountains, they
like there to hear the birds singing and the father
is seeing this. And he thinks, I will take the birds
from the mountains and put them in the people's houses
so they can hear the singing always. And he does.
So even in the poorest houses there is this little
gold cage with the bird in it. And the father sees
the birds need seeds to eat, so he sells these too.
Because he loves the birds. So when he must come to America
he must hire all of a ship to put his birds in. And two
thousand they are, singing in the cages in the hold.
And when he gets there he must give his business a new name
for his family to remember the mountains where the birds came from.

But in America no one is buying the birds and the son
sees this and says to the father: Birds don't sell.
So the son takes over the business though he is still a young man.
And everything is changing. The son brews soap
for the dog's bath, he mixes the powder to rub
on the cat's white belly, he grinds up the dead fish
to feed to the live ones that shimmer like glazed canaries
in the tanks. He is still a young man and he
is rich. He can make the dogs dance and sing
on television. He can sell the people mice and mouse food. But
it is not enough. Because he remembers the birds.
So he must buy that last gold stretch of land near the city
and hold it in the nest of his fist.

Swan Song

*In the last days of his life, Schubert
was frequently delirious, during which
time he sang continuously.*
—FISCHER-DIESKAU,
Schubert's Songs

The text caught in his blood.
Conceived in one quick sure
burst, it bloomed like a flower
no one understood.

This music was too pure
for the piano. Half-dazed friends
hearing it ascend
like a thin smoke climbing air

wept at the headboard. Hands
dithered, tired heads shook
on their necks, a scrollwork clock
beat time. The perfect sounds

kept drifting like an ache
from friend to friend. His joy
was lifting him away
from memory: the bleak

inconclusive days,
dull work, complaints, the nights
whirling at last to the streets,
their moments of sudden ease

and dawns. His blurred sight
resolved itself: let
those mourning angels fret
in the ring of their pain, complete

the escaping tune. He shut
them out. But the dizzying run
of their shared life kept the friends
blind, tottering in orbit.

All Shook Up

Elvis couldn't twitch a hip
or Ed would get the sack,
so they bundled his dream thighs
in flabby charcoal slacks

and tried to keep the cameras high
while Ed paced in the wings,
glaring at the monitors
where Elvis snarled, beading

sweat on a curled lip. Four
aging sharkskin crooners hummed
chords to muffle the beat,
blurred in swing harmony like some

USO group, sweet
as Karo. The fat microphone
was too far off to grab,
the slung guitar he'd brought from home

was cut off at the strap, the drab
curtain just waited to drop.
So did Ed. His really big show
was floating at the top

of Eisenhower Sundays. Who could know
the tiny screens would pop,
the cloth-smothered speakers split with the news
that we were all shook up?

Klumb's Rise

Klumb was cow-faced. Skin porous,
a play-doh gray, thick-lidded
eyes dull as those old pennies
we flattened on a track. Flunked
grades back, he began his move
in third: a year made him twice
the size of us,
              and, oddly,
good on the pole. His flat hands
two sandpaper mittens, he'd
reach up for each hot new grip.
From mats we'd watch sweat dripping
off the tight backs of his thighs
as they writhed him up, higher
than we could dare.
                  One winter
he clambered to the girders
so fast hardly anyone
noticed. His legs capped the pole
like the last hand on a bat,
his long arms free at last. He
clapped his palms like a monk, flipped
way back, turned, hung,
                    hit the mat.
The middle-aged gym coach fetched
smelling salts from a secret
room. We propped Klumb's heavy, wet
head in our laps and were glad
to see the fat cow eyes flap
open. We couldn't believe
anyone would go that far.

Family Album

You are turning the black pages
in the living room. There's no one there.
Each leaf, heavy and stiff,
dredges the still river of air,
hangs at its apex, then drops
you back into another age.

The black door shuts. You are just five,
huddling on a Lake Erie beach
between the two walls of your parents.
The glare makes you all smile, each
face the same pale overblown
balloon. Nobody seems alive.

Now a birthday. Combed and posed,
you glower under a paper hat.
Another party shot: that teen-age
summer you started getting fat,
caught with a Coke by the poolside
in your two-piece, overexposed.

As night comes on, the aging child's stare
darkens. You never earned
what your parents' cheap lens framed,
held and called the past. You turn
the black pages that lie on the air
of the living room. There's no one there.

Policies

TO MY FATHER

His green Nash gleamed, a scarab in the snow,
scuttling the plowed streets glazed from a half-melt
for contacts. The briefcase, stuffed and expectant,
would bounce like a small boy on the front seat.
Man talk in narrow steamed parlors, weak
coffee and fountain pens. Before Grandpa rose,
rebuttoning his brown-striped double-breasted coat,
he'd have the policy signed and filed away,
another life on paper.
                        Sharp, dead white
against the oak glare of the dining table,
forms filled your Sundays, the blank lines and rows
of figures demanding, as he did: Check,
Correct, Connect. Somehow it never took.
Nights after homework you'd rifle through tins crammed
with bright resistors, varied as butterflies.
Solder smell, dust scorched on glowing tubes,
cigarette smoke.
                  I remember the pinup
in the ham shack, burn holes in your work clothes,
the line of used black Fords, our family car.
After school once, perched in your swivel chair,
I broadcast to the whole world through the dead
microphone. Wet snow came down while you
sifted new surplus. CQ, CQ, you'd call
long after we were in bed, trawling waves
of night with a net of air.

                              Fierce, intricate,
that calling, when I think back, seems to hold
and blur the whole house like a blizzard.
Grandpa turns into static. We both watched
as he lost contact. On the last visit
he gave me a manly look, pumping my hand
as if I were his client. Cataracts
iced up his eyes. After he'd gone, you let
the policies on both of us expire.

Bay Window in a Rented House

FOR GEORGE

Remember that bay window
where we put the landlord's couch?
The panes had been painted shut,
Bert's "boy" had stippled the glass
with marble-hard globs. But a slice
of light still fell on the rose-colored
upholstery each fading afternoon.

It was frustrating. The only break
in those walls where he'd whitewashed over oak
was the set of sealed panes. In their frames
they reached out to catch heat and light
in a western arch. There were times
I'd doze off before supper on the still
warming air captured in that room.

I remember dreaming once of the house's
first owners: their dark wood, breezes,
and glimpse of the Bay before neighbors.
I woke up with the sunset in the roof lines
and looked out at the frame house next door
as always, the cluttered twilight
driveway, the rosebush half in bloom.

Leaving California

Now we are picking blackberries in the summer
hills. Plump, big as thumbs, they
plop in the tin bucket, building a soft
pincushion of skin, pulp and seed.
Below, the porch lights of Ashland
twinkle on like the first twilight stars.
I think of the dawn this morning, how the gold sun
split haze, then parched us on the freeways . . .
Redding, rows of Denny's, burnt-out
mountains, dammed-in Lake Shasta, stuffed with silver trout
and speedboats. In the late half-light
my picking hand looks gorged with purple blood.
Dark thorns coil and writhe between my tightened calves. Still
more fat berries gleam on their whiplike vines, still
more. We didn't leave California looking for
blackberries. But, finding them, we worked an hour
to harvest this side of a rich man's fence.
Our filled pails are heavy and sweet. Behind the green wall
a nervous horse snorts, neighs, and stamps.

The House Destroyed by Fire

Arrangement preserves. The way a calm tureen
of fish soup hubs our circle or a stripped oak
table anchors its room. Order, unseen
at first, settles like fine ash. Our talk
glimmers. A candle set behind glass
fences the crickety dark.
                           Not knowing what
went first, I have to imagine chaos:
a tongue licking out from the wood stove that
hissed *kitchen* all day, a spark in the new
socket chasing its wire like a fuse,
rags waking to a slow smolder below
the floorboards. More details sprout—quick shadows
jagging papered walls, the rows of spice tins
exploding, reams of typing like wild
cabbages of flame.
                        Once it's begun,
description stuffs itself sick. That charred field,
blanched by now, is probably filled with bugs.
The fieldstone lattice that cut out each odd square
of room has faded under weeds. Only dregs
remain: littered, still tantalizing, as the fear
of loss grows ragged, peculiar, seedy.
Spare work set our table, arranged the taste
that opens that time now. Let memory
give way to bare articulate space.

A Priest of Aphrodisias

Winched up from gray rubble,
I rock the air. Rope-draped,
dangling chains from my shoulders,
I might be a slave or a man
wrestling with snakes. I am neither.
No laurel fringe on my brow
but two rings, taut as muscle,
gleaming. The goddess I serve
knew to preserve the texture
of my features. Blank, delicate
as madrepore, my eyes never
blink. My stone lips are perfect.
Only my nose has suffered
the insult of history: a pox
of celibates, troubled
by its fine arch. Propped on rods,
I look patched together.
I will not balance. My robe,
a froth of marble, cannot cover
my true weight. Laved in earth
or poking upright in the air —
I recognize neither as better.
That my right forearm has been lost
does not matter.

The All-Night Rumba

The bracelet she dropped on the beach
with Emilio after her
turned into dreamy Rio. Such
highways of light, such diamond towers—

the white city sang like a shell.
Moonlight shanties scratched at the edge
of the charmed circle, invisible
as sand. And when she wouldn't budge,

not one more step, the leopardskin coat
she threw down, pouting defiance,
was the forest, dark in its heat:
the great snakes sleeping on the vines,

the spiderleg root of river, huts
on its root hairs, small hungry fish,
shrubs in the mud. Emilio's touch
wormed up her fingertips to the wrist,

along her lank arm, then ringed her waist
like a moat. The suede belt that slipped
from her skirt to the moonlit coat sliced
the road to Brasília. Its sleek tip

pierced to the white heart of the place:
the city inside the dark. There
electricity throbs the veins and knees
dance to the nightstick's call. The air

is humming with short breaths. Cries tumbling
from darkened rooms flood into song—
she feels the sweet beat as they rumba
samba rumba all night long.

III

Election Day, 1849

Because the greatest beauty
is the death of a beautiful woman
the short man reels through the dawn.
The bells are warbling
their own endless poems
he has proven are impossible to write.
Too long, too long, he mumbles,
but still the turgid song
keeps stirring up words from the gray soup
of his brain. Titles
and the labels of bottles
are prancing in a ring, conjuring
Atlantis. Is that what the bells announce?
And these three men in the morning bar
ambassadors of beauty.

History will wring him clean
like a washcloth.
But first the sponge is soaked full
and the ringing day names him
repeater. Beauty has freed him
from politics: he votes again
and again for the man
whose men stand him
whiskey, prop him up along
the long strolls to the whirling
polls, where the curtain
falls again and again till it
drops for the last time like
a dishrag and he drops
in a gutter in Baltimore.

Settlement

Dawn seeps from the east
as storms drive up the west,
rumbling over the plains
like the buffalo in dreams
new townspeople once had here,
stalled before the frontier.

Thick yellow light fills in
a valley resembling the Rhine
more each day. A fat river winds
west under half-clouded skies.
Coopers, hog merchants and barge clerks
are stumbling down to work.

Their midday pints of beer
shimmer in sweating air,
while posted bills declare
opportunities most ignore.
That feather bed of sky
covered wagon trains yesterday.

Clouds, beat into a storm,
can look like huge beasts with horns
or ghost ships, cowled in sail,
on a dirt sea. The working day done,
the men would start home again
through a familiar rain.

Reggae Music

Until our people live again,
then I'm not satisfied.

This reggae music. The sun
squinting through a drift of frangipani,
the bland lagoon, the glinting bay,
shanties ringed like a tin

choker round the city's neck.
Motor sputter music. Hills
dangled with winding tentacles
of road, buses, a lurching bike—

all heading for the heart. Hot light
swings on the blare of a radio.
Poor Raymond starts to work on the new
city boys, easing that first long wait

for a handout, hustling the mountain weed
he needs to live. Gulls caw.
Faded, Deliverance Is Now
peels off a billboard staring at the street

from a rooftop, bright banana skin
peeking through the shreds. Jah sees
it all. In the sweet smoke fingering leaves
of shade, he builds a slow smile on

the mounting beat. His locks
dangle, rust-dulled coils of tin
in a sprung mane. The Lion
is thin. Wavering, he stalks

a glazed world. But Raymond's day
rocks steady now. Fat fruit
simmers in the market, new hits
soothe his transistor, the sea

delivers ships in its perfect blue
hands. Visitors start to sing
as they hit the coast, shacks disappearing
to a jungle view. The roads that go

back to the hills are sweltering in slick
oil coats. Bauxite sweats in the clay.
Dead men, lifting it out to the day,
lift to reggae music.

Peddler

IGOR FYODOROVICH STRAVINSKY 1882–1971

Scores in a drawer, waiting for a patron
or a grant, blank spaces on the staves,
just the beats inked in, the rhythm — rhythm
always comes free. And always it pulses back,
back to a past or dream of one: the small
estate, cottages around it like a charmed ring,
birches, and peasants you must have believed
you loved, their stiff dances, myths, Easters,
weddings, strawberry kvass combed in their hair.

Four pianos, gongs, wood blocks, chimes dangling
from frames, and the workmen: neat pianists,
percussionists — those cool technicians — tightening
the skin of tympani under the hushed
thrust of Russian from the chorus. I heard
that piece four times. On the last drive back
from Palo Alto each rich bungalow
we passed seemed to throb with the beat, and I
couldn't stop thinking of my wife's mouth, singing.

She told me the words appeared first in French,
translation had to take it back. I doubt
you'd have cared. Through Paris and New York
you stepped into different tongues like slippers,
sly peddler. On L.A.'s first amazing
freeways twining like runners round a tenant's
door, no one was native — you might have felt
at home. But at the bottom of your pack
the charm kept glistening, silent, like a gift.

Who will buy? The night they opened that new hall
named for a tissue-paper czar, you looked
too frail to stand. A movie-star alumnus
introduced you: hunched, cream-colored, pocked
with stubble, bowing to our standing applause
like a mushroom. The cantata began. Mouths
thrust around words the freed beat caught, and back,
those huts and peeling trees, again the old gift
sold—I'm ready to buy anything.

At the Concert

FOR CATHRYN

All through the summers of the endless nineteenth century
the German Lied was fattening like a prize steer.
Johannes Brahms brought Schubert's calf to market.
That Wunderkind died young, but the chubby man
kept lighting another stogie each New Year's.

This piece is a platter of beef, aged, marbled
with layers of harmony, set out before me. The piano's
as big as a house, the chorus full enough to fill
a stockyard. There you are: a face at the crowd's edge,
mouth, eyes, round forehead, hair my hands know.

Alto. Hidden inside the Lied, you're singing
what I just half hear. I'm back in the kitchen—
the somber tune you hummed there ribs this melody
with minors, makes deep chords dark and sweet. Brahms' old song
can reach me now. You make the century rich.

Alma Mater

I remember the dull thud of the chopper blade,
the glinting badges plucked off at a command,
the tac squad in powder-blue jumpsuits — that band
of avenging Papas — the jagged barricades
of bayonets, each jittery hand
on its trigger, the cameras, lies that made
the news each day, crowds, clouds of pepper fog sprayed
from squad cars down the streets where we made our stand.
Our feet never touched the ground. Sweet mother,
you had us. Helpless, dangling from your paps
over that pit, we plotted in dorm rooms, deferred
and stoned, put off papers, scudded on scholarships.
When the blind fathers whipped us toward history,
how could we leave you to grow up and die?

Lamento

SALVADOR ALLENDE GOSSENS   1908–1973

When I saw that last picture in an old Sunday paper
I couldn't help but think of North Dakota . . .
dawn in an early fall, cold radio voices between the ads
on WDAY, the barren plain at the top of gray
America stretching out forever, going nowhere.

In the grainy newsphoto you looked bestial,
a snub-necked panda in spectacles and helmet,
backed against the rock wall for a fight. You call
dead telephones. You search a white, droning sky. You clutch
the automatic rifle that Fidel won the revolution with . . .

ages, ages ago. Today I read,
Foreign observers give the four-man junta high marks
for seeking pragmatic solutions to the chaos. Pinochet
yawns from a slick *Newsweek* photo, his plump wife
beaming like a pumpkin. No, *the generals*
are not Fascists; in fact they have no serious dogma other
than a rather infantile anti-Marxism.
Salvador, the babies brought you down!

Salvador, they made the municipal stadium their playpen,
stuffed five thousand prisoners in for a birthday party.
When Victor Jara sang Neruda's songs for the thirsty crowds,
guards came and stomped his hands, cracked his guitar
across his head, strangled him with nylon strings for a joke, and then
they shot him. You couldn't hear the laughter. You were dead.

The President glares at the crowds in the stands
at half time in the TV room. He worries about the image
on the tube, stares in the mirror during commercials,
scribbles illegible cryptic notes on a yellow legal pad.

The cold voice of the Secretary of State Security
drones pragmatic solutions into a phone. Subversion and insurgency,
maintaining credibility, is hard work. He yearns
for the gentlemen's diplomacy of the nineteenth century . . .
emperors and open wars, ambassadors in frock coats,
the small pistol in the velvet-lined train car.

Ambassadors with stars on their shoulders step from the American jet,
shake hands with old teachers from West Point and the Pentagon,
walk into a white room to meet with representatives
of copper interests talking of recompensation. *The copper mines,*
which account for 80 per cent of Chile's export revenues,
are producing at the highest rate in the nation's history.

The President strolls on the white beach, carefully slicing
gray air with his right hand. He talks of copper and
the economy, soda pop and oil, united fruit and national
security. A measured bass tone projects
confidence, no-nonsense pragmatism, no serious
dogma other than a rather infantile anti-Marxism.
His toddler-general audience grins and coos.

Pablo Neruda in a seashore house circled
by soldiers, dying because he is old, dying
because he cannot get the right medicine to calm
the cancer that sears him, dying because the white cells
keep eating the pink ones, keep feeding and growing and
are never satisfied. At the highest rate
in the nation's history he is dying. The coils
of the Anaconda crush out the life.

There are few dangerous snakes in North Dakota—a handful
of rattlers hiding in sandstone caves. Salvador, the rim
of this nation is a landscape you would not recognize. Here
only a few Norteamericanos seek pragmatic solutions
to the chaos. Foreign ambassadors give them high
marks for the booming industry, the well-paved
tank-wide roads, the ivory silos beneath the earth stuffed
with quiet death. We have no need of medicine.
The lair of the Anaconda is hidden.

Stretching out forever, going nowhere under the delicate waist
of America, recompensated copper mines export shiny
revenue. Fruit boats, fat as flies, chug coffee and bananas
to our doors. Eighty per cent of trade with Chile has now been
restored. But Isla Negra, broken Chile, Victor Jara
with his hands crushed black—what can recompensate
for them? Silent in the sunrise haze,
a nameless Indian drops off a pier
like a piece of dead fruit dropped on the rot pile.

Dawn in an early fall. On the barren plain
at the top of America I heard that you had died
between the ads. Salvador, I drove on, and now near where I write
the Esmeralda squats on a rotting bay. Your photograph
has gotten frail as parchment with age. The yellow paper
curls like the dried wing of a butterfly.

Learning to Clam

On the cold coast west out of Hoquiam,
I'm a stalker with a short-handled gun,
looking for dimples in damp sand to scoop out
and slosh in. Clamming is watching,
your close friend said, as we raced here under
a rising fog. But my own clam-eye's
unfocused like a baby's, and the dawn-gray beach
gets littered with caved-in holes until
I learn to see under sand.
                            That strange tug
of life and then release as the numb hand
pulls the razored shell through a suck of mud,
after three hours it almost becomes
familiar. The backs of my shoulders remember
the bite of that bent-up shovel, my palms
are marked with the grain of its handle.
The gritty catch clatters in our bags
all the long way back.
                        In the barnlike
kitchen we learn to slice off guts, wash
the ribbony innards in the sink. A bucket
fills with brittle hunks of shell, clean parts
plop in a mixing bowl. Dipped in flour now,
the milk-colored meat is turning gold in oil.
I catch a whiff of ocean off the pan. Clam
steam fogs up all the windows, enclosing us
like memory.

Pioneer Square

Boundaries: the wrought-iron pergola,
clothesline boxing rings around tables,
a three-decker parking lot shaped like a wedge
of pie. Land ends here. The last rich coast,
last chance. Drunks are snoozing on green benches
beneath Chief Sealth's totem. Carved in rock,
he gives the block his best noble Indian
stare. It doesn't work. Those warehouse cafés
still clump along the street, new antique shops
parade their fire horns and fishing nets,
while the brick rocket of the Smith Tower
keeps on prodding the sky, which doesn't fall.

He can't be blamed for giving up his name.
What the hell, he must have thought, the country
was going to the dogs anyway.
The century stood half-empty, and besides,
Sealth was rich: islands clustered to the west
like August blackberries, the rivers frothed
salmon. After he'd vanished into cliché,
no one was certain just whose chief he was—
some potlatch tribe, no doubt, all gifts and boasts,
a grandiose purveyor of humped-up
oratory. Florid, rhetorical,
his speech, translated, still insinuates.

Tribe follows tribe, and nation follows nation.
The pipeline bums are rising from their dreams
of lost Alaska. Instamatics freeze
them to the picturesque. The Smith Tower
goes on shooting one man's last chance at the sky
above Sealth's stone frown—the century
can never end. Inside the nineties bars,

all brass and beveled glass, the down vests glow
on the coatracks, the first beers froth, as the day
sinks west and work ends. Weekends fill
the ferry lanes. Everybody's leaving
for the islands, everyone's flying away.

The Court Painter

Prince Don Baltasar Carlos on Horseback

Here is the prince's head, perched like a cloud
on a velvet stump. His liver-colored horse,
set against a heroic sky, looks fierce,
but coldly fierce — both prince and steed are posed
for the statue they'll eventually become.
The court painter, an old hand at his craft,
paints in the boy's gold glove a cut-off staff
that counters his mount's rising to a run.
Energy and control. The prince's sash
balancing mane and tail, the way the beast
is carefully shrunk by a third — down to the last
detail the court painter can please with such
cold skill only the eyes hint that the king's son
is on a merry-go-round he has outgrown.

The Drunkards

Everyone's drunk. Ha. Each oily face
looks like a bloated goatskin bota bag.
Cheeksacks. Tongue a hungry finger, mouth a jug,
eye the mouth of a glimmering jug. Bacchus
lolls belching. His puffy boy pours the wine,
keeps an eye out for newcomers, crowns
a supplicant with vine leaves. Every man's
a king. Everybody's having a good time.
Hands curling tight round a cup or stretching out
the way a beggar reaches out for bread
are caught in light. The painter has arrayed
them like arrows pointing to the neat
moral he knows will charm the king. It works—
a hundred ducats pour into his purse.

Don Diego de Acedo

A certain refined taste for the grotesque
is, like hemophilia, the result
of delicate breeding. To enjoy the faults
of nature—the odd hump or limp, the mask
of ugliness hiding a cutting wit,
the old man bulging out a child's body
like an ill-fitting suit—requires some study
of classic models, a connoisseur's eye, and tact.
The painter can satisfy each quirk of taste
like a master chef. Swathed in official black,
with royal ink and quill, an unwieldy book
on his knees, the dwarf secretary waits
for greatness. His cocked hat and blank, rude
stare show the cold refinement in his blood.

The Royal Family

It is all done with those mirrors, of course:
the one the court painter paints on the back wall
of the scene, where the parents look regal
in reflected light as if they were the source
of everything, and the invisible glass
he uses to paint himself painting. The pose
he has chosen shows him for what he is
trying to show: a clear eye, wit, and craft.
Ironically, the subjects of this piece
are bystanders. The Infanta, her two maids,
attendants, and dog, look on as he paints
the royal parents. With all the ruffled sleeves,
false flowers, silk, that horde of girls and scarves,
it is hard to tell the princess from the dwarfs.

Don Juan de Austria

The essence of this art is mimicry.
Beneath a general's plume, sash and black silk,
the aging jester does his job. The tilt
of his half-bald head and the tight, nubbly
fist gripping the staff reveal his grasp
of the task at hand: to keep the perfect pose
his role demands and still make it show
the absurd contrast. The painter does the rest.
Tools of the trade—helmet, sword, breastplate—
are strewn at the jester's feet in a mockery
of martial pride, or old fools, or maybe
art. The challenge comes in filling out
a shell with your tools—easels, brush and oils
might just as well be rattles, cap and bells.

The Surrender of Breda

When empires start to fall, they start to build
palatial retreats. The king's small hunting lodge,
lined with Rubens' nudes, can take the edge
off the wearisome cares of state, while the walled
Palace of Good Retirement brags glories:
sieges, standard triumphal equestrian
scenes, surrenders from all over, a salon
of monarchs, some labors of Hercules.
This one has all the king requires, yet
odd details leap out — that smoldering camp,
all those pikes, a horse's rearing rump,
tired chaos of soldiers glaring out
dead center. Even in retreats, the painter
can do more than just one more surrender.

Pope Innocent X

Innocent, great, captured in full face,
fills out the frame inside a scarlet sea
of robe. The collar at his throat holds sway
like a whitecap, while the spattered froth of lace
that tries to hem things drifts out, fluttering
on waves no one can see. Beyond the swell
floats flesh: an ear shell, cocked eye of a gull,
a crabbed hand crawling — *You may kiss the ring.*
The painter did. He knelt before the throne
to catch that rush of light at just the right
angle and made the sign of the cross straight
through the face: the Pope's nose slicing down
into mustache. Painting is a prayer
to power, the frame a sea wall against fear.

Portraits of the King

Forty years with the boss's face: that mound
of pale Austrian flesh still foreign as snow,
eyes a cloudy, half-thawed puddle the nose
divides, a drift of chin, those puffed lips bland
as worms, and hung just over them the thin
ruby wings of the mustache taking off—
he knows it all, yet always finds the stuff
of kings inside that withering sack of skin.
It gets harder. Each stroke is a memory,
each smudged bag under the drooping eye
reminds him that this weary model's life
is sagging down with his own, that mastery
can fade like majesty. But not yet: the last
flattering portrait flatters the painter best.

The Tapestry Weavers

There is a myth behind this one. Displayed
on the back wall in a tapestry for sale
Ariadne pleads with her lover. Will
it sell? Those ladies peering at the thread
in front and the knots in back look skeptical.
Still, desertion appeals and the poor girl's dressed
almost as well as they. It might have just
the right effect spread over a bedroom wall.
The painter has one staring out front, toward
those others: barefoot, in a workshop light
that coats their limbs like sweat. He sets a cat
snoozing among balls of twine, shows tools—wool card,
wheel, hand spindle—and draws the stare to its end
focused on the weaver's moving hand.

About the Author

After the Splendid Display is Don Bogen's first book, but he has already won the first Edwin Markham Award of the Eugene V. Debs Foundation (1976), the Discovery Award from *The Nation* (1980), and Grand Prize in the AWP Anniversary competition (1982). Bogen studied at the University of California, Berkeley (A.B. 1971, Ph.D. 1976). He is associate professor of English at the University of Cincinnati.

About the Book

After the Splendid Display has been composed in Bembo by Annie Graham Publishing Services. It was printed on 60 lb. Sebago. It was printed and bound at Kingsport Press. The jackets and covers were printed by Phoenix Color Corporation. It was designed and produced by Joyce Kachergis Book Design and Production.